D0273916

Table of Contents

Who Am I?

I live in the trees, eating green leaves.

I have a black nose and long claws on my toes.

My big ears are furry. And I'm not in a hurry.

Who am I?
A koala!

2

Koalas

Laura Marsh

NATIONAL
GEOGRAPHIC

Washington, D.C.

For Elizabeth, Madison, and Kaitlin — L.F.M.

Special thanks to: Deborah Tabart, OAM, CEO of the Australian Koala Foundation;
Susan Kelly, Director, Global Briefing (www.koalahospital.com); and the Koala Hospital in Port
Macquarie, NSW, Australia (http://www.koalahospital.org.au).

Copyright © 2014 National Geographic Society.
This British English edition published in 2017
by Collins, an imprint of HarperCollins*Publishers*,
The News Building, 1 London Bridge Street, London. SE1 9GF.

Browse the complete Collins catalogue at
www.collins.co.uk

All rights reserved. No part of this publication may be reproduced, stored in a retrieval system,
or transmitted, in any form or by any means, electronic, mechanical, photocopying, recording
or otherwise without the prior permission in writing of the publisher and copyright owners.

A catalogue record for this publication is available from the British Library.

ISBN: 978-0-00-826664-6
US Edition ISBN: 978-1-4263-1466-7

Book design by YAY! Design

Photo credits:

Cover, AP Images; 1, Kitch Bain/Shutterstock; 2, Gerry Pearce/Alamy; 4–5, Image100/Jupiter Images/Corbis; 6, Anne Keiser/
National Geographic Creative; 8, Pete Oxford/Minden Pictures/Corbis; 9, Yva Momatiuk & John Eastcott/Minden Pictures; 10, Theo
Allofs/Minden Pictures; 11, Eric Isselée/Shutterstock; 12, Clearviewimages RM/Alamy; 13, Esther Beaton/Taxi/Getty Images; 14–15, Daniel
J Cox/Oxford Scientific RM/Getty Images; 16, Robert Harding World Imagery/Getty Images; 17, surabhi25/Shutterstock; 18 (UPLE),
manwithacamera.com.au/Alamy; 18 (UPRT), LianeM/Shutterstock; 18 (LO), Flickr RF/Getty Images; 18–19 (background), Africa Studio/
Shutterstock; 19 (UP), L. Clarke/Corbis; 19 (CTR), Kitch Bain/Shutterstock; 19 (LO), AnthonyRosenberg/iStockphoto; 20 (LE), D. Parer &
E. Parer-Cook/Minden Pictures; 20 (RT), Diana Taliun/Shutterstock; 21, Bruce Lichtenberger/Peter Arnold/Getty Images; 22, Flickr RF/
Getty Images; 23, shane partridge/Alamy; 24–25, Neil Ennis/Flickr RF/Getty Images; 26, Susan Kelly/Global Briefing/www.koalahospi-
tal.com/www.koalahospital.org.au; 26–27 (background), Shutterstock; 27 (UP), Joel Sartore/National Geographic Creative; 27 (CTR),
Susan Kelly/Global Briefing/www.koalahospital.com/www.koalahospital.org.au; 27 (LO), Joel Sartore/National Geographic Creative;
28, Ocean/Corbis; 29, Thiess/Hardman Communications; 30 (LE), Bruce Lichtenberger/Peter Arnold/Getty Images; 30 (RT), Image100/
Jupiter Images/Corbis; 31 (UPLE), Kevin Autret/Shutterstock; 31 (UPRT), Ventura/Shutterstock; 31 (LOLE), Sam Yeh/AFP/Getty Images; 31
(LORT), roundstripe/Shutterstock; 32 (UPLE), Gerry Ellis/Digital Vision; 32 (UPRT), tratong/Shutterstock; 32 (LOLE), K.A.Willis/Shutter-
stock; 32 (LORT), Markus Gann/Shutterstock; header banner, Shutterstock; Tree Talk koala, Shutterstock

Printed and bound in China by RR Donnelley APS

MIX
Paper from
responsible sources
FSC™ C007454

FSC
www.fsc.org

This book is produced from independently certified
FSC™ paper to ensure responsible forest management.

For more information visit: www.harpercollins.co.uk/green

Where Koalas Live

PACIFIC
OCEAN

Koalas live in a country called
Australia. They live in forests and
wooded areas. They live in the
mountains and on the coast.

Pouch Animals

Koalas look a little like teddy bears. But they are not bears at all.

Koalas are mammals called marsupials. They carry their babies in pouches. Kangaroos and wombats are marsupials, too.

baby in pouch

wombats

Tree Talk

MAMMAL: An animal that feeds its babies milk. It has a backbone and is warm-blooded.

MARSUPIAL: A mammal that carries its babies in a pouch

kangaroos

Built to Climb

A koala's body is perfect
for living in trees.

Its body curls up to fit between branches.

Fur on its bottom is extra thick. It is a built-in cushion!

Long arms wrap around trees.

Strong legs help a koala climb up and down trees.

Paws have pads that keep a koala from slipping.

Long claws dig into tree trunks and branches.

Front paws have two thumbs and three fingers. These help grab branches.

Life in the Trees

Koalas are good climbers.
They spend most of their time in trees. This is their habitat.

Koalas sleep in trees, too.
They doze off in some funny places.
Could you sleep like this?

Koalas are slow and sleepy. They sleep up to 18 hours a day.

Tree Talk

HABITAT:
An animal's
natural home

A koala lives in a small area in its habitat. The area has about 100 trees. This is its territory.

Male koalas have a scent patch on their chests. They rub it on the trees.

scent patch

This tells other koalas to stay out of their territory.

Tree Talk

TERRITORY: An area where an animal or group of animals eats, travels, and lives

Picky Eaters

Koalas eat lots of eucalyptus leaves. But they only eat from a few kinds of eucalyptus trees.

To get enough food, koalas eat for about five hours every day. Koalas mostly eat and sleep.

eucalyptus leaves

6 Cool Koala Facts

1

Koalas can jump from tree to tree.

2

Koalas hardly drink any water. They get most of their water from leaves.

3

A koala's fur protects the animal from the heat, cold, and rain.

4

Koalas are very active at night.
They like midnight
snacks!

5

Koalas have
fingerprints, just
like we do.

6

Eucalyptus leaves smell like
cough sweets. Koalas
do, too!

Baby Koalas

A baby koala is called a joey. When it's born, it does not have any hair. It is also blind.

The joey stays in its mother's pouch for about six months. It drinks milk and grows bigger and bigger.

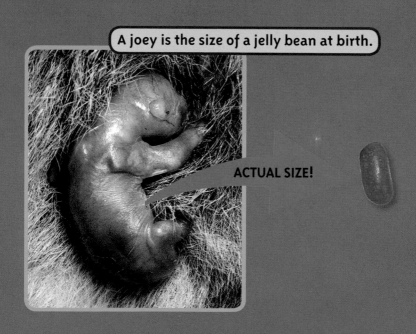

A joey is the size of a jelly bean at birth.

ACTUAL SIZE!

A joey peeks out of its mum's pouch.

Soon the joey comes out of the pouch. It hangs on mum's chest or rides on her back.

The young koala learns how to climb and hang on so it can live safely in the trees.

Q Why do koalas carry their babies on their backs?

A Because they can't get a buggy up a tree.

23

In Danger

Today koalas and people often have to share space.

Koalas need
land with trees.
But people are
cutting down trees
to make farms,
roads, and buildings.
There is less land
for koalas. They are
in danger.

Koalas get hurt,
too. They get hit
by cars or hurt
by pet dogs.

Helping Koalas

Luckily for koalas, there are hospitals just for them.

Doctors and nurses help koalas that are sick or hurt. Koala hospitals help thousands of koalas every year.

A koala gets help after it was hit by a car. It will be taken to the Koala Hospital in Port Macquarie, New South Wales, in Australia.

This koala's arms were hurt. The casts help them heal.

Hospital workers give loving care to a sick koala.

This koala is being weighed.

Koalas get help in other ways, too. Road signs tell drivers to watch out for koalas.

NEXT 10 km

Q Why did the koala cross the road?

A Because it was the chicken's day off.

A koala uses a tunnel that goes under a road.

Tunnels and bridges can help koalas cross roads. But koalas don't always know where the safe places to cross are.

Saving eucalyptus trees is the best way to help koalas. Trees are homes for koalas.

What in the World?

These pictures show close-up views of things in a koala's world. Use the hints below to work out what's in the pictures. Answers on page 31.

HINT: A marsupial carries her baby in here.

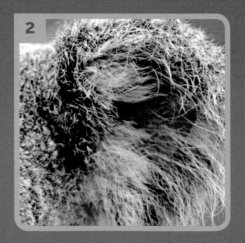

HINT: You have two of these, but they are not furry.

WORD BANK

leaves　claws　pouch　trees　joey　ears

HINT: This is a koala's favourite food.

HINT: These help a koala climb.

HINT: It lives in a pouch after its birth.

HINT: A koala spends almost all of its time here.

Answers: 1. pouch, 2. ears, 3. leaves, 4. claws, 5. joey, 6. trees

HABITAT: An animal's natural home

MAMMAL: An animal that feeds its babies milk. It has a backbone and is warm-blooded.

MARSUPIAL: A mammal that carries its babies in a pouch

TERRITORY: An area where an animal or group of animals eats, travels, and lives